D0239594

I ♥ Craft

...TTING

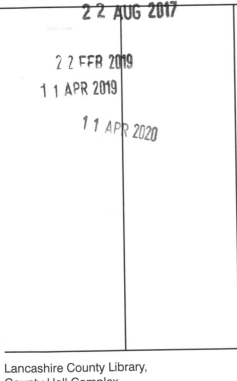

This book should be returned to any branch of the
Lancashire County Library on or before the date shown

2 2 AUG 2017

2 2 FEB 2019

1 1 APR 2019

1 1 APR 2020

Lancashire County Library,
County Hall Complex,
1st floor Christ Church Precinct,
Preston, PR1 8XJ

www.lancashire.gov.uk/libraries

Lancashire
County
Council

LL1(A)

Rita Storey

W

LANCASHIRE COUNTY LIBRARY

30118134794613

Franklin Watts
This edition copyright © Franklin Watts 2017
All rights reserved.

Copyright © Franklin Watts 2014
All rights reserved.

Dewey classification: 746.4'32'043

ISBN: 978 1 4451 5496 1

Packaged for Franklin Watts by Storeybooks
rita@storeybooks.co.uk
Designer: Rita Storey
Editor: Sarah Ridley
Crafts made by: Rita Storey
Series editor: Sarah Peutrill
Photography: Tudor Photography, Banbury
www.tudorphotography.co.uk

A CIP catalogue record for this book is available
from the British Library.

Printed in China

Cover images: Tudor Photography, Banbury

Franklin Watts
An imprint of Hachette Children's Group
Part of The Watts Publishing Group
Carmelite House
50 Victoria Embankment
London EC4Y 0DZ
An Hachette UK Company
www.hachette.co.uk
www.franklinwatts.co.uk

FSC
www.fsc.org
MIX
Paper from
responsible sources
FSC® C104740

Before you start

Some of the projects in this book require scissors, glue, a safety
pin or a tapestry needle. When using these things we would
recommend that children are supervised by a responsible adult.
Please note: keep homemade toys and products
away from babies and small children.
They cannot be tested for safety.

Contents

Before You Start

Knitting is a way of making fabric by joining together lots of loops. The loops can be made on your fingers, on a machine or using knitting needles.

Attention!

If you are left-handed, read on. Some people who are left-handed prefer to knit as right-handed people. Try that first. Others prefer to swop all the instructions to the opposite hand.

Knitting needles

Knitting needles come in different sizes. The smallest is 2mm and the largest standard size is 10mm. Big needles are used with thick yarn to make chunky fabric. Small needles are used with thin yarn to make fine fabric.
In this book the crafts use 4mm and 6mm needles.

Yarn

Yarn comes in different thicknesses (weights). Yarn can be made of wool, cotton, silk, flax and man-made fibres.
* 3 ply
* 4 ply
* double knitting
* Aran
* chunky
* super chunky
In this book the crafts use double knitting, Aran, chunky and super chunky yarns.

A tapestry needle with a big eye is useful for sewing up your work.

double knitting

Aran

chunky

super chunky

Casting On

To begin knitting with needles you need to make some stitches. This is called **casting on**.

1 Leaving an 8-cm tail of yarn, loosely knot the yarn onto a knitting needle (A). If you know how to do a slip knot, do that instead.

2 Slide needle B through the loop and underneath needle A, as shown.

3 Wrap the yarn around needle B, as shown.

4 Pull the yarn down between the needles.

5 Slide the right-hand needle (B) down and back towards you, picking up the loop of yarn that is lying between the needles. Now needle B is on the top.

6 Put the loop of yarn on needle B onto needle A, to join the first loop stitch. Take out needle B.

7 Pull the yarn tight (but not too tight) and slide needle B through and behind the top stitch. Repeat steps 3 to 6 to make another new stitch.

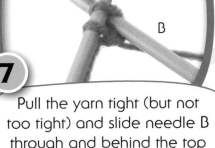

8 Repeat steps 3 to 7 until you have as many stitches as you need.

Finger-knit Brooch

Make a fashion statement with one of these simple finger-knit brooches. Wear it on a hairband (see pages 8 – 9), on a bag, or simply pin one or more onto a sweater or coat for a fashion accessory that is 'right on trend'.

To make one brooch you will need:

* 2m of Aran yarn cut from a 50g ball
* fabric glue and spreader
* circle of card, 4cm across
* duct tape
* safety pin
* scissors
* a craft jewel

loop

length of yarn

tail (loose)

1 Knot the yarn loosely onto the first finger of your left hand. If you know how to make a slip knot, do this instead.

tail

2 Hold the tail of yarn in between your second finger and your thumb.

yarn

3 Put the length of yarn over the back of your finger and let it hang down, as shown.

4 Lift the loop stitch that you made in step 1 over the yarn and drop it over the end of your finger.

5 Hold the tail between the finger and thumb of your right hand. Pull it gently until the loop is tight. Keep making more loop stitches by repeating steps 3, 4 and 5 until the finger knitting measures 25cm.

6 Slip the loop off your finger. Leaving a 10-cm tail, cut the yarn. Pass the cut end of the yarn through the loop. Pull it tight. Trim both of the loose ends.

7 Paste glue onto the circle of card. Press one end of the finger knitting onto the centre of the circle.

8 Wind the knitting around in a spiral. Press in place. Leave to dry.

Make some more for your friends!

9 Turn the card over. Tape a safety pin in the middle of the card, as shown (left). Turn the brooch over. Glue a jewel onto the centre of the brooch.

Finger-knit Hairband

Keep your hair neat and tidy with this funky finger-knit hairband.

You will need:

* 1 x 50g ball of super chunky knit, multicoloured yarn * scissors
* 2 x 10-cm lengths of ribbon

1   2   3
        4

thumb
        palm

1 Hold the end of the yarn between your thumb and finger 1, letting the tail of yarn trail across your palm.

2 Wind the yarn over finger 2, under finger 3 and over finger 4.

3 Wind the yarn around finger 4. Then go back the other way, over finger 3, under finger 2 and over finger 1. You should now have yarn on fingers 1, 2, 3 and 4.

4 Follow steps 2 and 3 again. You should now have two rows of yarn on fingers 1, 2, 3 and 4.

5 Starting with finger 4, take hold of the yarn at the base of the finger. Pull it over the other loop of yarn on that finger and over the end of your finger. Do the same with fingers 3, 2 and 1.

6 Repeat steps 2, 3, 4 and 5 until the knitting is long enough to fit across your head, from ear to ear. The knitting will look like the picture above.

7 To finish off, put the loop of yarn on finger 4 onto finger 3. Lift the bottom loop on finger 3 over it and off your finger.

8 Put the loop left on finger 3 onto finger 2. Lift the bottom loop on finger 2 over it and off your finger.

9 Put the loop left on finger 2 onto finger 1. Lift the bottom loop on finger 1 over it and off your finger.

10 Slip the last loop off your finger. Cut the yarn 5cm away from the knitting and pass the end through the loop. Pull it tight.

11 Thread a piece of ribbon through the knitted hairband, near to one end. Tie in a knot. Repeat on the other side.

You could decorate your hairband with one of the brooches from pages 6 – 7.

French Knitting Necklace

French knitting is done using a simple machine called a dolly instead of knitting needles. Make this French knitting dolly to create a pretty necklace.

1 Use the ruler to measure 2.5cm along each lolly stick and make a mark with the biro.

You will need:

* 4 lolly sticks
* biro * ruler
* sticky tape * scissors
* empty kitchen-roll tube, cut in half
* wrapping paper
* 1 x 50g ball of double knitting yarn
* cocktail stick or knitting needle
* 3 beads with a 4mm hole
* 2 x 25-cm lengths of 1-cm wide ribbon

2 Tape each lolly stick to the kitchen-roll tube, lining up the biro marks with the end of the tube. Make sure that the lolly sticks are evenly spaced around the tube.

3 Cover the tube with the wrapping paper and tape in place. Now you have a French knitting dolly!

4 Thread the end of the yarn through the dolly to create a tail.

5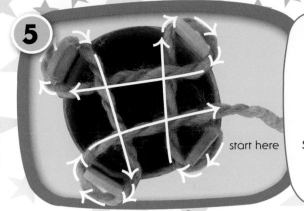

start here

Wind the yarn around the lolly sticks by following the arrows in the picture on the left. Repeat. There should now be two loops of yarn on each stick.

6 Use a knitting needle or a cocktail stick to lift the bottom loop over the top loop on each stick. Tug on the tail to tighten.

7

Keep repeating steps 5 and 6. The French knitting will start to appear at the bottom of the tube. Stop when the knitting is long enough to fit around your neck.

8

3 4 3

1 2 2

To finish off, place the next loop (stick 1) onto stick 2. Lift the bottom loop on stick 2 over it and off the stick.

Put the loop left on stick 2 onto stick 3. Lift the bottom loop on stick 3 over it and off the stick.

Put the loop left on stick 3 onto stick 4. Lift the bottom loop on stick 4 over it and off the stick.

9 Slip the last loop off the stick. Cut the yarn 5cm away from the knitting and pass it through the loop. Pull it tight.

10 To finish the necklace, thread the knitting through the beads. Tie each piece of ribbon through the ends of the knitting. To fix the necklace around your neck, tie the ribbons in a bow.

You can use the French knitting dolly again and again.

11

Scarf

A simple knitted scarf can be turned into something really special by adding a multicoloured fringe. And no one else will have one quite like it!

You will need:

* 1 x 100g ball of purple chunky yarn
* 1 x 50g ball of blue chunky yarn
* 1 x 50g ball of green chunky yarn
* pair of 6mm knitting needles
* scissors * tape measure
* tapestry needle

1 Cast on 25 stitches (see page 5).

2 Knit rows of garter stitch until the scarf is 80cm long. If you need to learn how to knit, turn to page 26.

3 Cast off (see page 28).

To make a longer scarf, knit more rows (step 2). You may need more yarn though!

4 To make the fringe, cut three 40-cm lengths of blue yarn. Cut one 20-cm length of green yarn.

5 Lay the three lengths of blue yarn together. Tie them together half way along, using the green yarn.

6 Thread both ends of the green yarn through the eye of the tapestry needle.

7 Push the point of the needle through the end of the scarf, 1cm in from the long edge and one knitting row up from the end of the scarf.

8 Pull 5cm of the blue yarn through the scarf. Untie the green yarn.

9 Feed the ends of the blue yarn through the loop and pull tight, as shown.

10 Repeat steps 4 to 9 with purple yarn. Repeat steps 4 to 9 with green yarn. Add more fringes all the way along the short edge.

11 Repeat steps 4 to 10 to make an identical fringe at the opposite end of the scarf.

Mittens

Keep snug this winter with a pair of trendy fingerless mittens.

To make a pair of mittens you will need:

* 1 x 50g ball of super chunky yarn

* pair of 4mm knitting needles

* tapestry needle * scissors

* pencil and paper (for tracing the template)

* orange felt * blue felt

* fabric glue * 2 buttons

tail

1 Cast on 24 stitches (see page 5) leaving a 20-cm tail. (This will be used to sew up the mitten in step 4.)

2 Row 1 – Knit two stitches (see page 26), purl two stitches (see page 27). Repeat to the end of the row. Repeat this row three more times (rows 2 – 4). This is called double rib.

3 Row 5 – Knit all the stitches in this row.
Row 6 – Purl all the stitches in this row.
Repeat rows 5 and 6 until the knitted fabric measures from your wrist to just above your knuckles.
Cast off (see page 28). Cut the yarn leaving a 10-cm tail (this will be used to sew up the mitten). Thread the tail through the last loop and pull tight.

B

A

4 With the flat side on the inside (see photo), fold the rectangle of knitted fabric in half along its longest side. Thread the tail of yarn (A) through the tapestry needle. Now turn to page 30 to see how to oversew. Use this stitch to sew half way up from the ribbed end. Fasten off. Using the tail of yarn (B), oversew a quarter of the way down from the top. Fasten off. There will be a gap between the two lines of sewing for your thumb. Turn the mitten the right way out.

thumb opening

5 Repeat steps 1 to 4 to make a second mitten.

6 Trace the template on page 31 and use it to cut out two orange flowers and two smaller blue flowers from the felt.

7 Glue a blue flower in the centre of each orange flower.

8 Glue a button onto the centre of the blue flower. Glue the flowers onto the back of each mitten.

Owl Family

Make these adorable owls as a special gift for a friend. But will you be able to give them away?

For the family of owls you will need:

* 1 x 50g ball of chunky multicoloured yarn

* pair of 4mm knitting needles

* scissors * tapestry needle

* fabric glue

* square of light-brown felt

* square of white felt

* 4 black buttons, 5mm across

* 2 black buttons, 12mm across

* square of orange felt

* toy stuffing from a craft shop

* paper and pen (for tracing the template)

These owls look just like me!

1 To make the small owl you will need to knit two rectangles and join them together. Cast on 10 stitches (see page 5) and knit 12 rows of garter stitch (see page 26). Cast off (see page 28). Repeat to create a second knitted rectangle.

2 Place one knitted rectangle on top of the other and join them along three sides by oversewing them (see page 30).

3 Fill the middle of the knitted pocket with toy stuffing. Oversew the remaining side.

4 Trace the eye templates on page 31. Use them to cut out two of the larger circles from the light-brown felt.

5 Cut out two of the smaller circles from the white felt.

6 Glue a 5-mm button onto each of the small white circles. Glue a white felt circle onto each of the two light-brown circles to make eyes.

7 Glue the eyes onto the top corners of the knitted owl body.

8 Trace the beak template on page 31. Use it to cut out a small orange beak from the felt.

9 Glue the beak onto the knitted owl between the eyes.

10 To make a medium-sized owl, cast on 15 stitches and knit 15 rows. Repeat to create a second knitted rectangle. Follow steps 4 to 9 using the templates on page 31 for the medium-sized owl.

11 To make a large owl, cast on 20 stitches and knit 22 rows. Follow steps 4 to 9 using the templates on page 31 for the large owl. Use the 12-mm buttons for the centre of each eye.

17

Woolly Mice

You won't hear a squeak out of these colourful little pets. That makes them perfect to live in your pocket.

For one mouse you will need:

* 1 x 50g ball of double knitting yarn
* pair of 4mm knitting needles
* toy stuffing from a craft shop
* 2 small black beads * ruler * glue
* tapestry needle * pink felt * scissors
* 8-cm length of white double knitting yarn
* pencil and paper (for tracing the template)

Mmmm. I like mice (only joking!).

1 Leaving a 20-cm tail of yarn, cast on 25 stitches (see page 5). Knit three rows of garter stitch (see page 26).

A

B

2 Row 4 – Slide the right-hand needle (B) through the second and third stitch on the left-hand needle (A), as shown above. Knit the two stitches together. Knit along the row to the last two stitches.

A

B

3 Slide the right-hand needle (B) through the last two stitches on the left-hand needle (A), as shown above. Knit the two stitches together.

4 Keep knitting more rows, repeating steps 2 and 3 until you have just three stitches left. Knit the first stitch. Knit the second and third stitch together. Knit the remaining two stitches together. You should have one stitch left on your needle.

5 Cut the yarn leaving a 30-cm tail. (This will be used to sew up the mouse.) Thread the tail through the last stitch loop and pull tight.

6 Thread the tapestry needle onto the 30-cm tail. Oversew (see page 30) along the long edge. Stuff the body of the mouse with toy stuffing.

7 Using the 20-cm tail, sew a line of running stitches (see page 30) along the open edge. Pull the stitches tight. Sew three stitches, one on top of the other, to stop the mouse body from coming undone. Trim the loose end to make a tail.

8 Trace the template on page 31 and use it to cut out two ears from the pink felt. Fold and glue the pointed end of each ear. Leave to dry. Using the photo on the right as a guide, glue the ears in place.

9 Thread the tapestry needle with the white yarn. Slide the needle half way along the yarn. Push the needle and the doubled yarn through the mouse's nose. Snip off the needle by cutting through the loop.

10 Glue an eye on each side of the nose end of the mouse, between the ears and the whiskers, as shown.

Patchwork Cushion

Practise your knitting skills and make a great looking cushion at the same time.

1 Using purple yarn, cast on 16 stitches (see page 5). Knit 20 rows of garter stitch (see page 26). Cast off (see page 28). Repeat to make three knitted squares in this pattern.

You will need:

* 1 x 50g ball of purple double knitting yarn

* 1 x 50g ball of blue double knitting yarn

* 1 x 50g ball of cream double knitting yarn

* pair of 4mm knitting needles

* tapestry needle

* blue fleece fabric 19cm x 19cm

* cushion stuffing from a craft shop

* scissors

2 Using blue yarn, cast on 16 stitches. Knit two stitches (see page 26), purl two stitches (see page 27). Repeat until you reach the end of the row. Repeat this row 19 more times. This pattern is called double rib. Cast off. Repeat to make three knitted squares in this pattern.

3 Using cream yarn, cast on 16 stitches. Row 1 – Knit one row of garter stitch. Row 2 – Knit the next row in purl stitch. Repeat these rows nine more times. This pattern is called stocking stitch. Cast off. Repeat to make three knitted squares in this pattern. The photo below shows the squares with their right side facing up.

This looks like a comfy cushion for my nest!

4 Take one of each colour of knitted squares. Thread the tapestry needle with blue yarn and tie a knot in the end. Place the blue square on top of the right side (see step 3) of the cream square. Use running stitch (see page 30) to join one side of the blue square to one side of the cream one. Open them out. Repeat to join the purple square to the row, as shown.

5 Repeat step 4 to create another row of knitted squares. This time, place the cream square on the left of the row, the purple in the middle and the blue on the right.

6 Repeat step 4 with the last three squares. This time place the purple square on the left of the row, the blue in the middle and the cream square on the right.

7 With right sides together, oversew (see page 30) the three rows of knitted squares together to make one large patchwork square. The photo shows the underside of the patchwork squares.

8 Lay the patchwork of knitted squares face down on the right side of the piece of fleece fabric. Using small running stitches, join the two together by sewing along three sides of the square, 5mm from the edge.

9 Turn the cushion cover right side out. Fill with cushion stuffing. Oversew the last side to complete.

21

Mini Bunting

Brighten up your room with a row of these bright flags. They make every day feel like a celebration.

You will need:

* 1 x 50g ball of lilac double knitting yarn
* 1 x 50g ball of pink double knitting yarn
* 1 x 50g ball of yellow double knitting yarn
* 1 x 50g ball of blue double knitting yarn
* 1 x 50g ball of purple double knitting yarn
* pair of 4mm knitting needles
* 9 coloured beads with a large hole through the centre
* 5 small beads with a large hole
* 50cm of 1cm-wide ribbon
* scissors
* tapestry needle

1 Choose which yarn you will work with first. Leave a 10-cm tail. Cast on 15 stitches (see page 5). Knit three rows of garter stitch (see page 26).

2 Row 4 – Knit the first two stitches together (see picture above left and steps 2 and 3, page 18). Continue to knit until there are only two stitches left on the row. Knit the last two stitches together (see picture above right). Repeat rows 1 – 4 until you have three stitches left in the row.

3 Knit two stitches together. Knit the remaining stitch. On the next row, knit the two remaining stitches together.

4 Cut the yarn leaving a 30-cm tail. Thread the tail through the last loop and pull tight.
Repeat steps 1 to 4 to make five knitted flags in different colours.

5 Using the tapestry needle, thread a large bead onto the tail of each knitted flag.

6 Thread a small bead below the large bead. Tie a knot to keep the beads in place. Trim the yarn.

7 Fold over the top of a flag by 1.5cm. Thread the 10-cm tail through the tapestry needle and sew the edge of the flap with running stitch (see page 30).

8 Thread the tapestry needle with ribbon and feed it through the flap on each flag, adding a bead between each one.

Striped Purse

Make this cute purse to keep your pocket money safe. The pretty button and loop will stop the coins from falling out.

You will need:

* 1 x 50g ball of blue Aran yarn
* 1 x 50g ball of white Aran yarn
* pair of 4mm knitting needles
* tapestry needle
* scissors * ruler
* flower button

Follow steps 2 – 3 to make the scarf on pages 12 - 13 striped rather than plain.

1 Using blue yarn, cast on 15 stitches (see page 5). Leave a 20-cm tail.
Row 1 – Knit all the stitches (see page 26).
Row 2 – Purl all the stitches (see page 27).
Row 3 – Same as row 1.
Row 4 – Same as row 2.

2 Cut the blue yarn, leaving a 10-cm tail.

3 Leaving a 10-cm tail, begin knitting with the white wool. Knot the blue tail and the white tail together. Repeat rows 1 – 4 in white yarn.
Change yarn colour again and repeat until your knitting has five blue stripes and four white stripes.

4 Continue in blue yarn, knitting two stitches together at both ends of each row (see steps 2 and 3, page 18). Continue until only three stitches remain.

5 With just three stitches left in the row, knit two together and knit the final stitch. On the final row, knit the two stitches together. Cut the yarn and pass it through the loop. Leave a 5-cm tail. Cut off all the other tails along the side.

6 With the wrong side of the knitting on the outside (see picture) fold up the bottom third of the knitting. Thread the tapestry needle through the yarn tail and oversew (see page 30) down one side to form a pocket. Thread the tapestry needle with a 20-cm length of blue yarn. Oversew down the other side of the pocket.

7 Turn the pocket inside out. Thread the end of the 5-cm tail through the needle and form it into a loop. Sew two stitches to finish. Cut the yarn.

8 Sew the button onto the front of the purse. Use the loop on the purse flap to close the purse.

Knitting Stitches

Garter stitch

Once you have cast on some stitches (see page 5) you are ready to begin knitting.

1 Hold the knitting needle (A) with the stitches on it in your left hand. Slide the right-hand needle (B) through the first stitch and underneath the left-hand needle (A). Keep the yarn behind the needles.

2 Wrap the yarn around needle B as shown above. Pull the yarn down between the needles.

3 Slide the right-hand needle (B) down and back towards you, picking up the loop of yarn that is lying between the needles. Now needle B is on the top.

4 Using the right-hand needle (B), carefully slide the loop of yarn still on the left-hand needle (A) off the end of the needle.

5 Repeat steps 1 to 4 with all the stitches. This is called a **row**. Swop the knitting needles between your hands so that the needle with the knitting on it is in your left hand. Continue repeating steps 1 to 5 until your knitting is as long as you want it.

Purl stitch

Purl stitch takes a little more practice. Follow these simple steps to learn how to do it.

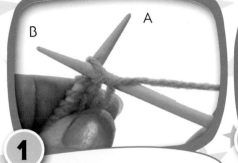

1 Hold the knitting needle (A) with the stitches on it in your left hand. Bring the yarn to the front. Slide the right-hand needle (B) down through the front of the stitch and in front of the left-hand needle (A).

2 Wrap the yarn around the tip of needle (B) as shown in the picture above. Pull the yarn down between the needles and to the front.

3 Slide the right-hand needle (B) down and back to pick up the loop of yarn that is lying between the needles to make a loop.

4 Slide the rest of the looped stitch off the end of the left-hand needle (A). Make sure the yarn is still at the front.

5 Repeat steps 1 to 4 to the end of the stitches. This is called a **row**. Swop the knitting needles between your hands so that the needle with the knitting on it is in your left hand. Continue repeating steps 1 to 5 until your knitting is as long as you want it.

Casting Off

Whe you have finished a piece of knitting you need to cast off, to stop it from unravelling.

1 Knit two stitches so that there are two stitches on the right-hand needle (B).

2 Slide the left-hand needle (A) through the far right stitch on the right-hand needle (B).

3 Use the left-hand needle (A) to lift the far right stitch over the other stitch, and off the end of the needle. This leaves one stitch on the right-hand needle (B). Pull the yarn tight.

4 Return to step 1 and knit another stitch so that there are two stitches again on the right-hand needle (B). Repeat steps 2 and 3. Continue until there is only one stitch left. Cut the yarn and pass it through the last stitch. Pull it tight.

Patterns

Knitting (see page 26) and purling (see page 27) are all the stitches you need to know to make many different patterns. These are the ones used in this book.

Garter stitch

In garter stitch, sometimes called **knit stitch**, every row is done using the same basic knitting stitch.

Double rib

To make a **double rib**, the number of stitches has to be divisible by 4. Follow these instructions:
Row 1 – Knit two stitches, purl two stitches, and repeat to the end of the row. Repeat until you have as much knitted fabric as you need.

Stocking stitch

In stocking stitch, you knit a row of garter stitch (see page 26), then a row of purl stitch (see page 27). Repeat until the knitting is the correct length. Stocking stitch gives a flat front (see the photo) but looks similar to garter stitch on the back.

Sewing Stitches

Running stitch

1 Push the needle through the fabric from the back.

2 Pull the needle and thread through to the knot.

3 Push the needle back through the fabric about 5mm away from where the thread came through.

4 Pull the thread through the fabric until it is tight, but not too tight.

5 Push the needle through from the back about 5mm away from the first stitch. Pull the needle and thread through and repeat along the length of the fabric.

6 Running stitch can be used to join two pieces of fabric or as decoration.

Oversew

1 Push the needle through the fabric from the back.

2 Pull the needle through to the knot. Pass the needle around the edge of the fabric and push the needle through the fabric from the back a bit further along.

3 Keep repeating to make more stitches.

Templates

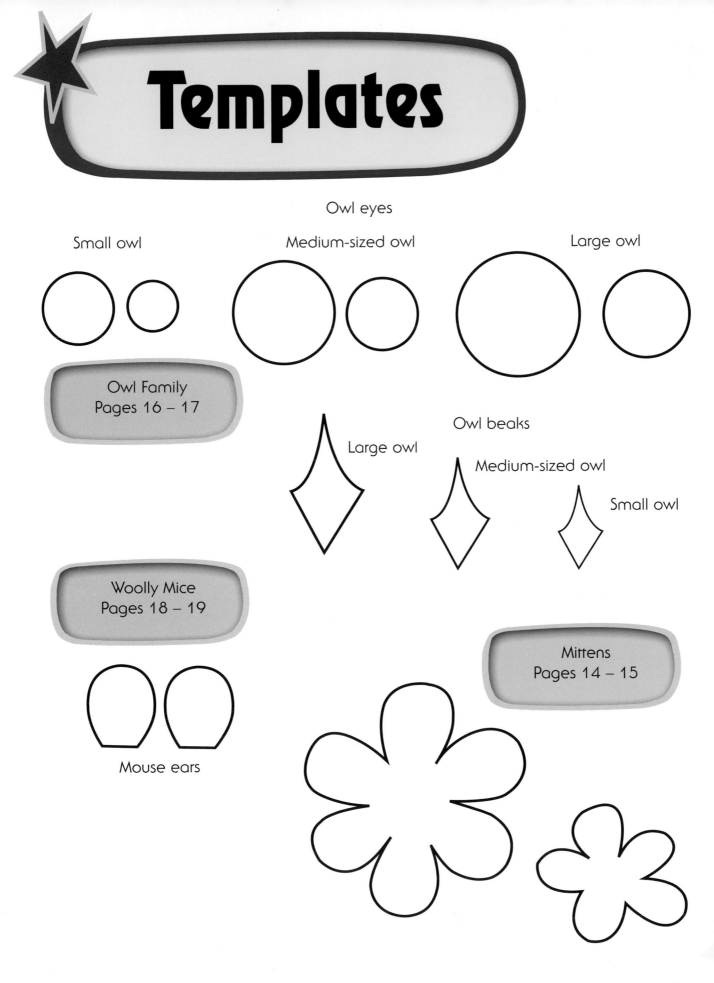

Owl eyes

Small owl

Medium-sized owl

Large owl

Owl Family
Pages 16 – 17

Owl beaks

Large owl

Medium-sized owl

Small owl

Woolly Mice
Pages 18 – 19

Mittens
Pages 14 – 15

Mouse ears

Index

Further Information

Websites

For short videos that demonstrate basic knitting stitches, go to: www.charlieandhannah.co.uk/knitting-videos

For more videos teaching people how to knit and crochet, go to: http://newstitchaday.com

For keen knitters, explore this Victoria and Albert Museum website: www.vam.ac.uk/page/k/knitting/